Figurative Photo

Bill Young
3302 E. La Salle St.
Colorado Springs, CO 80909
www.FigurativePhoto.com

Images available as prints: Please contact Figurative Photo for details.

Public law 111-40 is in the public domain.

ISBN 978-0-9895534-0-7

Published by: Ripple Effect Publishing LLC
Colorado Springs, CO
Designed in the USA
Printed and Bound in Korea

Going for the Gold!
The Congressional
Gold Medal
March 10th, 2010 WASP
Dedicated to my
Mother -
**Millicent
Amanda
Peterson
Young**
WASP
44-10.
A woman of
strength and
conviction!
By:
William
A.Young II
Kid Of
a WASP (KOW)

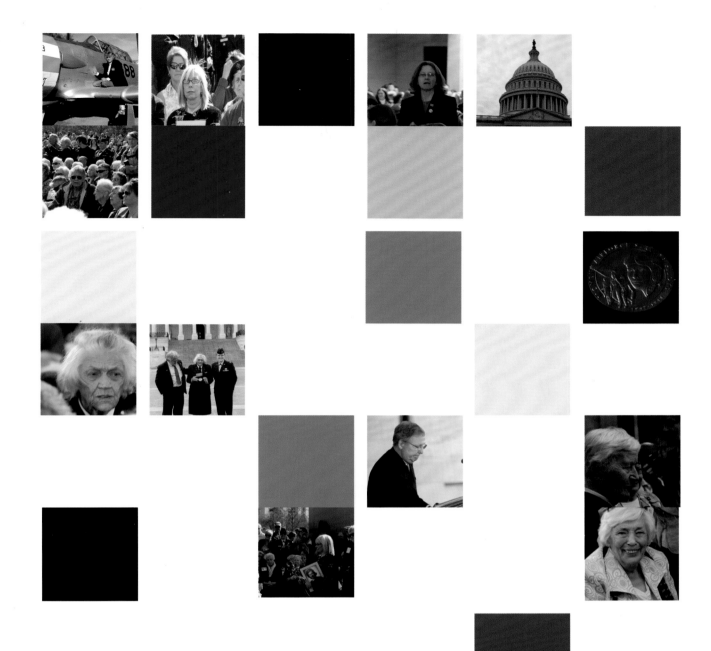

Going for the Gold is the Journey of
the Women Airforce Service Pilots
of World War II "WASP" on the way to receive their
Congressional Gold Medal and the events that took
place after the ceremony.

Table of Contents:

(The Congressional Gold Medal Journey)

March 2010, Washington DC. Spring is struggling to show itself, in one minute managing only wind and rain, the next bursting with sunlight, warm and full of promise. I've come east from the snow-laden Rockies with Millicent Young and her family. One of 170 women from around the country, Millicent has come to receive the highest honor this nation can give to civilians: the Congressional Gold Medal. Long before the ceremony begins the floor of the U.S. Capitol fills to overflowing, the crowds eventually swelling in a tight circle around the balcony of the rotunda - a sea of happy, expectant faces. In the very center of the hall is a cluster of gray-haired women, including Millicent Young, each one now in her eighties or nineties, some neatly dressed in their blue Women Air Force Service Pilot uniforms, many with walkers or wheelchairs. They are on this day a thousand fewer than they were at the beginning, some sixty years earlier, when they left their home towns and farms and families to answer their country's call, becoming pilots for the U.S. military during World War II. Out of 25,000 applicants, just over a thousand would be chosen for service. They would teach men to fly. They would tow targets behind planes to help soldiers practice gunnery skills. They would deliver aircraft across the country from factory to military field, including one or two models, like the legendary B-29 (later credited with winning the war) that in the early months no man wanted to fly. Now, six decades later, here in the nation's capitol, despite their years they look confident. They look proud. They look like Fly Girls. Still, despite the jubilant mood, in truth it's hard not to feel some regret that it has taken so long to acknowledge these women's service. During the War they had to pay their own way to Texas for training. And incredibly, for the thirty-eight who died during their tours of duty, family and friends would have to dig into their own pockets to pay for shipping home their loved one's remains. At the end of the War the women were summarily dismissed and sent home on their own dime, taking none of the usual military privileges - no GI Bill, no medical services at VA hospitals until the late 1970's. Unlike other service members, on their deaths the families of the WASP's were forbidden even to drape their coffins with the American flag, a cherished last rite for American veterans.

And yet here they are today - not bitter, but downright buoyant. By all appearances they're less concerned with past slights than with simply having a chance to celebrate their stories: Stories about how it felt to be part of a ground-breaking team of flyers.

About the thrill of piloting new planes right off the assembly line. And every now and then, stories that reveal a certain pride for having paved the way for thousands of other military women in the decades that followed. Indeed, at one point during the Gold Medal ceremony Air Force Lt. Col. Nicole Malachowski, the nation's first female Thunderbird pilot, rises to speak and makes this very point. As a young girl, she explains, people were quick to dismiss her dreams of becoming a fighter pilot. Then one day in a back room of the Smithsonian Museum she discovered a small display about the WASP. The history both moved and encouraged her, leaving her certain that with hard work she too could achieve what she yearned to do. It was the women gathered here in the center of the rotunda, she tells us, who redefined the possibilities for women looking to serve their country. After the ceremony I have the pleasure of helping push Millicent Young by wheelchair through the streets of Washington. The media has been covering the event in spades, and I soon lose count of the people who on seeing her in her uniform immediately come up - sometimes running across a busy boulevard to do so - to shake her hand and say thank you.

Young mothers stand on the sidewalks and excitedly introduce their daughters to her, telling them they owe women like Mrs. Young a thank you - not just for her military service, but for helping open roads that the daughters can now walk at will. Military enthusiasts ask for her autograph. During a ride on the subway a Boy Scout Troop stands up and launches into a cheer to honor her service. "Everyone talks about our sacrifice," Millicent tells me. "But for me it wasn't about sacrifice. I was making an investment - in myself, and in my country."

In 1977, shortly after women were first admitted into the Air Force Academy in Colorado Springs, the general in charge of the new female recruits announced to an assembled crowed that the time had finally come to see if women could fly the military way. Mrs. Young, who lived nearby and was sitting in the audience, stood up and raised her hand. "I believe that question has already been answered," she told him. Of course she was right, and what a pleasure it is to share this day with the women who settled that question; with these plucky, undaunted Fly Girls. Of course it's a relief to see their service finally acknowledged. But beyond that is the thrill of seeing them genuinely admired by the public at large. As if through their lives we've all gained a little pride, a little sense of the dignity that arises when courageous people meet the challenges of their times.

May the following pages, a beautifully crafted chronicle of the Gold Medal journey, take you to just such a place.

Gary Ferguson
January, 2011

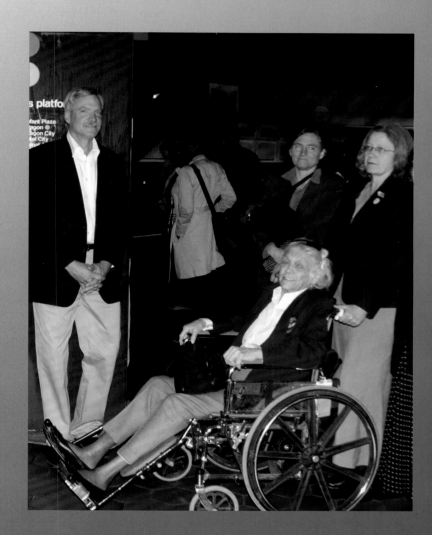

We didn't know it at the time but Back in November of 2008, the first real steps toward making the Congressional Gold Medal for the WASP a reality were put into play. I know that it was in the thoughts of many before that time but no real progress had been made.

Nancy Parish K.O.W. (Kid Of Wasp) and Director of Wings Across America was working with her mother Deanie Bishop Parrish WASP 44-W-4 to set up the fly girls exhibit at WIMSA. During that process they spoke with the first female USAF Thunderbird pilot Major Nicole Malachowski. Call sign "FiFi." Malachowski served as a White House Fellow and between the three of them they started the ball rolling to get legislation introduced for the WASP to receive the Congressional Gold Medal.

On March 17th, 2009 Senators Kay Bailey Hutchison and Barbara Mikulski introduced Senate Bill 614. All 17 female senators were original cosponsors!

Senator Barbara Boxer (D-CA)
Senator Maria Cantwell (D-WA)
Senator Susan Collins (R-ME)
Senator Diane Feinstein (D-CA)
Senator Kirsten Gillibrand (D-NY)
Senator Kay Hagan (D-NC)
Senator Amy Klobuchar (D-MN
Senator Mary Landrieu (D-LA)
Senator Blanche Lincoln (D-AR)
Senator Claire McCaskill (D-MO)
Senator Lisa Murkowski (R-AK)
Senator Patty Murray (D-W
Senator Jeanne Shaheen (D-NH)
Senator Debbie Stabenow (D-MI)
Senator Olympia Snowe (R-ME)

Senator Kay Bailey Hutchison

Public Law 111-40

111TH UNITED STATES CONGRESS
1ST SESSION

An Act
To award a Congressional Gold Medal to the Women
Airforce Service Pilots (`WASP').

Contents

SECTION 1. FINDINGS.

Congress finds that:

(1) The Women Airforce Service Pilots of WWII, known as the `WASP,' were the first women in history to fly American military aircraft;

(2) More than 60 years ago, they flew fighter, bomber, transport, and training aircraft in defense of America's freedom;

(3) They faced overwhelming cultural and gender bias against women in nontraditional roles and overcame multiple injustices and inequities in order to serve their country,

(4) Through their actions, the WASP eventually were the catalyst for revolutionary reform in the integration of women pilots into the Armed Services,

(5) During the early months of World War II, there was a severe shortage of combat pilots,

(6) Jacqueline Cochran, America's leading woman pilot of the time, convinced General Hap Arnold, Chief of the Army Air Forces, that women, if given the same training as men, would be equally capable of flying military aircraft and could then take over some of the stateside military flying jobs, thereby releasing hundreds of male pilots for combat duty;

(7) The severe loss of male combat pilots made the necessity of utilizing women pilots to help in the war effort clear to General Arnold, and a women's pilot training program was soon approved,

(8) It was not until August 1943, that the women aviators would receive their official name,

(9) General Arnold ordered that all women pilots flying military aircraft, including 28 civilian women ferry pilots, would be named "WASP", Women Airforce Service Pilots;

(10) More than 25,000 American women applied for training, but only 1,830 were accepted and took the oath,

(11) Exactly 1,074 of those trainees successfully completed the 21 to 27 weeks of Army Air Forces flight training, graduated, and received their Army Air Forces orders to report to their assigned air base,

(12) On November 16, 1942, the first class of 29 women pilots reported to the Houston, Texas Municipal Airport and began the same military flight training as the male Army Air Forces cadets were taking,

(13) Due to a lack of adequate facilities at the airport, 3 months later the training program was moved to Avenger Field in Sweetwater, Texas,

(14) WASP were eventually stationed at 120 Army air bases all across America,

(15) They flew more than 60,000,000 miles for their country in every type of aircraft and on every type of assignment flown by the male Army Air Forces pilots, except combat,

(16) WASP assignments included test piloting, instructor piloting, towing targets for air-to-air gunnery practice, ground-to-air anti-aircraft practice, ferrying, transporting personnel and cargo (including parts for the atomic bomb), simulated strafing, smoke laying, night tracking, and flying drones;

(17) In October 1943, male pilots were refusing to fly the B-26 Martin Marauder (known as the "Widow maker") because of its fatality records, and General Arnold ordered WASP Director, Jacqueline Cochran, to select 25 WASP to be trained to fly the B-26 to prove to the male pilots that it was safe to fly;

(18) During the existence of the WASP

(A) 38 women lost their lives while serving their country,

(B) Their bodies were sent home in poorly crafted pine boxes,

(C) Their burial was at the expense of their families or classmates,

(D) There were no gold stars allowed in their parent's windows; and

(E) Because they were not considered military, no American flags were allowed on their coffins,

(19) In 1944, General Arnold made a personal request to Congress to militarize the WASP, and it was denied; secrete, and filed

(20) On December 7, 1944, in a speech to the last graduating class of WASP, General Arnold said, you and more than 900 of your sisters have shown you can fly wingtip to wingtip with your brothers. I salute you... We of the Army Air Force are proud of you. We will never forget our debt to you.";

(21) With victory in WWII almost certain, on December 20, 1944, the WASP were quietly and unceremoniously disbanded;

(22) There were no honors, no benefits, and very few thank you's";

(23) Just as they had paid their own way to enter training, they had to pay their own way back home after their honorable service to the military;

(24) The WASP military records were immediately sealed, stamped "classified" or "secret", and filed away in Government archives, unavailable to the historians who wrote the history of WWII or the scholars who compiled the history text books used today,

with many of the records not declassified until the 1980s;'secret', and filed away in Government archives, unavailable to the historians who wrote the history of WWII or the scholars who compiled the history text books used today, with many of the records not declassified until the 1980s;

(25) Consequently, the WASP story is a missing chapter in the history of the Air Force, the history of aviation, and the history of the United States of America;

(26) In 1977, 33 years after the WASP were disbanded, the Congress finally voted to give the WASP the veteran status they had earned, but these heroic pilots were not invited to the signing ceremony at the White House, and it was not until 7 years later that their medals were delivered in the mail in plain brown envelopes;

(27) In the late 1970s, more than 30 years after the WASP flew in World War II, war;
women were finally permitted to attend military pilot training in the United States Armed Forces;

(28) thousands of women aviators flying support aircraft have benefited from the service of the WASP and followed in their footsteps;

(29) in 1993, the WASP were once again referenced during congressional hearings regarding the contributions that women could make to the military, which eventually led to women being able to fly military fighter, bomber, and attack aircraft in combat;

(30) hundreds of United States servicewomen combat pilots have seized the opportunity to fly fighter aircraft in recent conflicts, all thanks to the pioneering steps taken by the WASP;

(31) the WASP have maintained a tight-knit community, forged by the common experiences of serving their country during war;

(32) as part of their desire to educate America on the WASP history, WASP have assisted "Wings Across America", an organization dedicated to educating the American public, with much effort aimed at children, about the remarkable accomplishments of these WWII veterans; and

(33) the WASP have been honored with exhibits at numerous museums, to include--

(A) the Smithsonian Institution, Washington, DC;

(B) the Women in Military Service to America Memorial at Arlington National Cemetery, Arlington, Virginia;

(C) the National Museum of the United States Air Force, Wright Patterson Air Force Base, Ohio, to America Memorial at Arlington National Cemetery, Arlington, Virginia; United States Air Force, Wright Patterson Air Force Base, Ohio;

(D) the National WASP WWII Museum, Sweetwater, Texas

(E) the 8th Air Force Museum, Savannah, Georgia;

(F) the Lone Star Flight Museum, Galveston, Texas;

(G) the American Airpower Museum, Farmingdale, New York;

(H) the Pima Air Museum, Tucson, Arizona;

(I) the Seattle Museum of Flight, Seattle, Washington

(J) the March Air Museum, March Reserve Air Base, California; and

(K) the Texas State History Museum, Austin, Texas. United States Air Force, Wright Patterson Air Force Base, Ohio;

(D) the National WASP WWII Museum, Sweetwater, Texas;

(E) the 8th Air Force Museum, Savannah, Georgia;

(F) the Lone Star Flight Museum, Galveston, Texas;

(G) the American Airpower Museum, Farmingdale, New York;

(H) the Pima Air Museum, Tucson, Arizona;

(I) the Seattle Museum of Flight, Seattle, Washington

(J) the March Air Museum, March Reserve Air Base, California; and

(K) the Texas State History Museum, Austin, Texas

SEC. 2. CONGRESSIONAL GOLD MEDAL.

(a) Award Authorized.
The President pro tempore of the Senate and the Speaker of the House of Representatives shall make appropriate arrangements for the award, on behalf of the Congress, of a single gold medal of appropriate design in honor of the Women Airforce Service Pilots (WASP) collectively, in recognition of their pioneering military service and exemplary record, which forged revolutionary reform in the Armed Forces of the United States of America.

(b) Design and Striking.
For the purposes of the award referred to in subsection

(c), the Secretary of the Treasury shall strike the gold medal with suitable emblems, devices, and inscriptions, to be determined by the Secretary.

(d) Smithsonian Institution.

(1) IN GENERAL.
Following the award of the gold medal in honor of the Women Airforce Service Pilots, the gold medal shall be given to the Smithsonian Institution, where it will be displayed as appropriate and made available for research.

(2) SENSE OF THE CONGRESS.

It is the sense of the Congress that the Smithsonian Institution shall make the gold medal received under this Act available for display elsewhere, particularly at other locations associated with the WASP.

SEC. 3. DUPLICATE MEDALS.

Under such regulations as the Secretary may prescribe, the Secretary may strike and sell duplicates in bronze of the gold medal struck under this Act, at a price sufficient to cover the costs of the medals, including labor, materials, dyes, use of machinery, and overhead expenses.

SEC. 4. NATIONAL MEDALS.

Medals struck pursuant to this Act are national medals for purposes of chapter 51 of title 31, United States Code.

SEC. 5. AUTHORIZATION OF APPROPRIATIONS; PROCEEDS OF SALE.

(a) Authorization of Appropriations.
There is authorized to be charged against the United States Mint Public Enterprise Fund, an amount not to exceed $30,000 to pay for the cost of the medal authorized under section 2.

(b) Proceeds of Sale.
Amounts received from the sale of duplicate bronze medals under section 3 shall be deposited in the United States Mint Public Enterprise Fund.

Legislative History

* S. 614, (H.R. 2014)
* CONGRESSIONAL RECORD, Vol. 155 (2009):
May 20, considered and passed Senate.
June 16, considered and passed House.
President Obama signed it into Public Law 111-40 on July 1, 2009.

ORGANIZATIONS THAT SUPPORTED S.614

99's
AFA (Air Force Association)
American Legion
Association of the US Navy
Coast Guard Aviation Association
CAF (Commemorative Air Force)
EAA (Experimental Aircraft Association)
EANGUS (Enlisted Association National Guard)
Military Order of World Wars
MOAA (Military Officer's Association of America)
ROA (Reserve Officer's Association)
VFW (Veterans of Foreign Wars)
WMA (Women Military Aviators)
Discovery of Flight Foundation
WAI (Women in Aviation International)

Photo of President Obama signing the stimulus Bill on February 17th, 2009. Photo by Bill Young figurativephoto.com © 2009 Bill Young. Photo placed here to represent signing of the Congressional Gold Medal bill 111-40

After the announcement of the ceremony the KOW's
started making plans. It was a bit difficult as we didn't
know when the ceremony was going to take place. Some
of us thought it would take place in March just before
the congressional spring break. We believed it would be
in March as March is National Women's History Month.
We felt that this would be a good time for the congress
to go home and talk about the good things they had just done!

Others thought the ceremony wouldn't take place until
late October or early November so that they could bring
good news home just before the election. It is difficult to
plan for a big event when you don't know when it will
happen.

Congress took some amazing steps to support the WASP
One of them was to allow them to have a voice in what
the medal would look like. They sent e-mails out to
every WASP with samples that were pre approved by the
U.S. Mint. They were marked confidential and we were all
asked not to let the art samples get out. It only took a few
hours for the art to make the Internet.

By the end of November the bad news was rushing in. The WASP were dying in droves. It was estimated that only 280 were still alive. By the end of the year estimates were that only 269 were still alive and several others were in bad physical shape. With the youngest of them being 83 and several in their 90's it is no wonder that we were loosing them.

The KOWs pushed for the dates to be moved up, and make this happen as soon as possible. So we finally got a date and detailed instructions as to how things were going to happen.
The following e-mail's were sent out:

> The ceremony would be hosted by President Obama in the Rotunda of the Capitol building on March 10th. The medals may or may not be ready. On March 9th we would have ceremonies at the World War II Memorial for the laying of the wreath for the 38 fallen WASP, and then a ceremony at the Women's Memorial for a salute. Each WASP would receive two tickets for the Gold Medal Ceremony and lists would be made for all other guests to observe from other rooms via TV monitors.

> One Gold Medal would be ceremoniously presented to a member of the WASP and given to the Smithsonian Institutution. All other medals would be issued to individual WASP in a manner to be determined.

Fifinella (Fifi) was a gremlin designed by Walt Disney for a proposed film from Roald Dahl's book the Gremlins. The WASP asked permission to use the image as their official mascot. The Disney Company granted them the right. Many WASP had leather patches made with Fifi on them. Fifi was to protect the women pilots during the war.

Formal invitations to the official Congressional Gold Medal Ceremony on March 10, 2010, at 11 a.m., have been mailed to the WASP and designated family representatives of deceased WASP. Please be sure to RSVP to the Speaker of the house using the instructions included in the invitation.

Other celebration events include a Remembrance Ceremony at the World War II Memorial and a Welcome Salute Reception with senior Defense Department officials at the Women In Military Service For America Memorial.

These events will be held on the afternoon of March 9. On March 10, following the official ceremony there will be a Celebration Reception at the U.S. Capitol for WASP and their guests. We've put together a Celebration Activities Information paper (updated March 4th) about all of these events as well as other useful pieces of information to help attendees get a better picture of the two-day celebration. You may want to print a copy of the information paper and keep it with your travel information as a handy guide for event dates, times and locations. Also, you must print and complete the Reservation Form for these events and return it by Feb. 26, 2010. It is only necessary to com plete and forward one (1) Reservation Form per WASP family group. We understand this is a very quick but nec essary turn-around if all arrangements are to be made.

It may also be helpful to periodically review the listing of Qs and As that address various items related to the award of the WASP Congressional Gold Medal ceremony. We will update this listing as we get new information. You can also visit the Web site of Senator Kay Bailey Hutchison or the Wings Across America's Web site.

Information about discounted airline travel, accommoda tions and rental cars, as well as additional information re garding transportation, parking, etc., is included in the Cel ebration Activities Information Paper (updated March 4) and the Q & A listing."

The invitation, with two tickets and instructions arrived. Within minutes we were on the phone finding out who can make it for sure and setting specific dates of arrival and departure. We called the number on the invitation within a couple of hours and provided a list of 9 family members including my mother for the ceremony.

The Congress of the United States
requests the honor of your presence at a
Congressional Gold Medal Ceremony
in honor of

The Women Airforce Service Pilots

on Wednesday, the tenth day of March
two thousand ten, at eleven o'clock in the morning

The Rotunda
United States Capitol
Washington, District of Columbia

The favor of your reply is requested by February 26
(202) 225-5885
Speaker.RSVP@mail.house.gov

All Women Airforce Service Pilots are welcome to bring
family members and guests. For security purposes,
all guests planning to attend must R.S.V.P.

United States Congress

Admit Bearer

UNITED STATES CAPITOL
THE ROTUNDA

111TH CONGRESS
Congressional Gold Medal Ceremony
In honor of
The Women Airforce Service Pilots

March 10, 2010
Seating begins at 9:30 a.m.
Program 11:00 a.m.

NONTRANSFERABLE

Please bring photo identification and nontransferable ticket for entry
Seating available at nine thirty
Please arrive no later than ten thirty
North or South Visitors Entrance

Please be aware that seating in the Capitol Rotunda is limited
and will be available on a first-come, first-served basis.
Additional seating will be available as necessary.

Within a couple of days the rumors started that family members of the fallen 38 were not getting into the ceremonies, family members of living WASP were not getting in, and WASP themselves were not getting in because the venue was full. Panic spread across the e-mail list because others had invited as many as 72 guests, and they were all getting in. Some WASP with no family invited 20 guests, and yet children and spouses of WASP were not allowed.

Brigadier General Wilma L. Vaught, USAF (Ret.), sent out another message to put some of the rumors to rest. We quickly exceeded the venue in regard to attendance so things had to be changed, but they were still going to proceed with the ceremony in a way that accommodated the most people.

"Alert Change to WASP Celebration Events"
(Updated 03/3/10)

It seems that each time we make an update, it means we have had a change in plans for the WASP Congressional Gold Medal Celebration. Regrettably, this message is more of the same. We sincerely apologize for the turmoil this may have caused for you, your family and friends. The extraordinary enthusiasm of the WASP and their overwhelming response has caused us to exceed capacity in every venue. As a result, we have had to institute some restrictions with respect to attendance and seating, and in the case of the Remembrance Ceremony, a change in venue. The following addresses each of those changes:

* The Remembrance Ceremony, which is scheduled for 2 p.m., March 9, has been moved to the US Air Force Memorial, just above the Pentagon on Columbia Pike, Arlington, VA. The venue had to be moved from the World War II Memorial because the number of attendees far exceeded the limit permitted by the National Park Service. Everyone is welcome at this event at the Air Force Memorial but seating is limited to WASP and the WASP Representatives of the 38 who lost their lives in training and in the line of duty.

The Air Force Memorial's address is One Air Force Memorial Dr., Arlington, VA 22211. Parking is limited. The US Air Force Memorial is the newest in the family of national memorials in the DC area. The WASP were among the honored guests during the Memorial's dedication in 2006.

* Bus transportation for the Remembrance Ceremony will depart the Gaylord National Hotel at 1:00 p.m. As a reminder, WASP travel free and all others must pay $20 that will cover all bus transportation during the celebration. To assure we order enough buses, RSVP is required for all passengers - see Reservation Form on the Women's Memorial Web site.

* Following the ceremony, buses will transport WASP + two (2) guests and WASP Representatives + one (1) guest to the Women's Memorial for the Welcome Salute Reception. All others with bus passes may board the buses for return to the Gaylord National Hotel. We are making arrangements for a windshield tour of Washington, DC, during the return trip. The WASP representatives and their guests will be transported back to the hotel following the reception.

* As indicated in the above paragraph, we have had to dramatically curtail the number of guests attending the 4 p.m., March 9, welcome Salute Reception at the Women's Memorial. Even though we arranged for a large party tent on the Memorial Plaza to accommodate the enormous number of guests, we were still three times the capacity of the Memorial and the tent. The National Park Service has required us to bring the number into safety and security conformance. In order to assure we accommodate the WASP and the WASP Representatives as the first priority, we have had to limit attendance to WASP + two (2) guests and WASP Representatives + one (1) guest. This was an extremely painful decision but the best possible under the circumstances. While the Memorial will be closed to the public after 2 p.m. on March 9, it will be open 8 a.m. to 5 p.m. daily, for you to visit and to see the Fly Girls of World War II exhibit while you are in the area.

* As a reminder, the reception following the WASP Congressional Gold Medal Ceremony on March 10 has been cancelled. The decision had to be made to assure the safety and security of all attendees at the ceremony. The reception had to be cancelled in order to use the space for overflow for ceremony guests.

If you have not forwarded a Reservation Form to the Women's Memorial Foundation for the events on March 9, please call 800-222-XXXX/703-XXX-XXXX as soon as possible. You must have a bus pass in order to ride the bus. Event tickets are required for seating at the Remembrance Ceremony, and admittance and seating at the Women's Memorial Reception. We will package all bus passes and tickets for each of these events by WASP family group under the name of the WASP. The packages will be at the Gaylord National Hotel during the morning of March 9, until the buses depart for the Remembrance Ceremony at 1 p.m. Bus passes and tickets will also be available at the Women's Memorial during the March 9 reception.

"Thank you for your patience and understanding as we have worked to put together these events in record time. Our goal remains as it always has been, is to make this a great celebration for the WASP."

Brigadier General Wilma L. Vaught, USAF (Ret.) and her staff did an amazing job of putting everything together even though things changed from moment to moment. There were still some points of disappointment among the kids but, I didn't hear it among the WASP themselves and let's face it, this is all about the WASP!

This event turned out to be the largest event ever held in the capitol building! More than 3,000 people in attendance. The only things really lost in the process was the reception. And they didn't get everyone to witness the salute at the Women's Memorial.

We started to receive calls two and three times a day, giving us information about what was going to happen, when, and how!

We received a call and an e-mail from The Women's Memorial, informing us that American Airlines was going to give the WASP and their guests discounts on tickets, and that we should wait to hear from them before booking flights.

Later that day we received a call from Ms. Russell, informing us that the WASP were going to fly for free and that guests would receive a big discount! I think free tickets are great discounts. Thanks American Airlines!

Millicent Young and other WASP were received in Dallas by a reception, including pilots, community leaders, and Tuskegee Airmen recipients of the Congressional Gold Medal on March 29, 2007. Announcements of the WASP' arrival were announced throughout the building. Photos of WASP were posted at each gate, and on the carts that transported the WASP from the gate to a reception area, and then to the next gate to travel to Washington D.C. Once we arrived at the reception area we noticed my mother was sitting right behind a photo taken of her in 1944.

We were told that we could get discounts at the Gaylord National Hotel, and that the WASP would receive a $200.00 a night discount, and yet the price was still over $200.00. We found a hotel with rates in the $70.00 a night range. With 27 nights of bookings for our entire group that provided a significant savings.

We had free transportation to and from the Metro, and the staff always pointed out to other customers that they were in the presence of a Congressional Gold Medal honoree! You could see the pride on Benny's face as he drove us to and from the Metro.

American Airlines really pulled out all the stops for this trip. They moved us into first class. They announced to everyone on the plane that they were flying Millicent Peterson Young to Washington D.C. to receive the Congressional Gold Medal. They gave her flowers and people came up to be photographed with her. It was a very proud moment!

Mom with a flight attendant - They moved us to first class for the flight and both of the flight attendants came to have their photo taken with my mom.

Mom met the entire crew and a man came on the plane to give her a corsage!

Tuskegee airmen received the Congressional Gold Medal on March 29th, 2007. American Airlines arranged for one to meet my mother at the airport.

Dallas is the main hub for American Airlines. AA made a big deal of the WASP flying with them. They had about 30 people waiting at the gate for our flight. They had previous Congressional Gold Medal Honorees. Shuttles and desks with photos of the WASP on them and a bit of history. They announced over the loud speakers that they were coming in and ushered them around as if they were royalty. They provided them with a banquet room full of food and drinks, and allowed people to meet them as they moved throughout the airport.

Several women approached the WASP, crying and asking to hold the hands of a WASP, or to get a signature. Men and women thanked them for their service and stated how proud they were of them, and that they were receiving this recognition. Most of them said - "It's about time!" Kids looked on with amazement, wondering what it was all about, and people were trying to explain it to them. You would have thought rock stars had just arrived at the airport!

When we arrived in Washington D.C. family members were waiting to meet us. We were to arrive earlier than the rest of the family, but weather had delayed our flight.

Benny the driver from our hotel was honored to transport my mother each day. He gave us his home phone number in case we arrived when he was off duty. He wanted to make sure he was the one to pick us up each evening and make sure my mother had safe passage too and from the airport and the Metro stop. My mother and Benny saluted each other with respect. Benny had served our country in Vietnam.

The laying of the wreath took place at the Air Force
Memorial on a beautiful but hot day. The women I spoke
with were very pleased with the setting. The sculpture of the con-
trails shown bellow really gave the sense that flight was in action.

This ceremony was held to honor the 38 WASP that were killed
in service. A number of their family members, as well as living
WASP were in attendance.

The laying of the wreath for the fallen 38 was a sad moment as
a number of WASP and family members remember their fallen
loved ones and friends. The fallen 38 will never be forgotten
since they live in our hearts and souls.

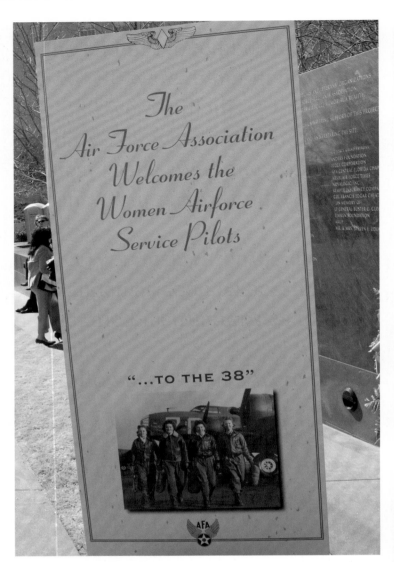

The
Air Force Association
Welcomes the
Women Airforce
Service Pilots

"...TO THE 38"

AFA

Love,
Honor,
Remember
the 38

The WASP gather at the Women's Memorial for the salute. The exhibit extended for this occasion was "The Fly Girls," put together by Nancy and Deane Parish. The exhibit was a wonderful display that traced the efforts of the WASP along with a photographic history. When this show is taken down, it will go on the road so that others may see it around the country. Look for it in your area or request it at a local museum.

Gathering at WIMSA to see the Fly Girls exhibit and receive the Parishs' new book!

51

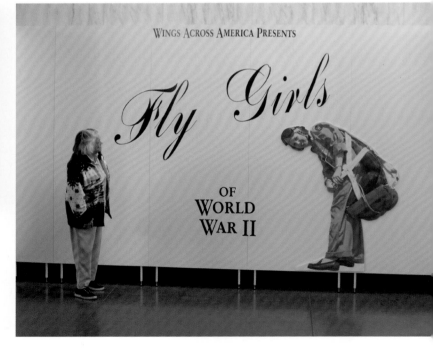

Eileen Collins, first female space shuttle commander, credits the WASP for being a pilot. General Schwartz said he wouldn't be a flyer today if it weren't for the WASP!

53

USAF Thunderbird pilot Major Nicole Malachowski. Call sign "FiFi" remembers going to the Smithsonian Air and Space Museum as a little girl, finding a display talking about the WASP, and deciding that she would be a pilot one-day!

The Big Day: March 10th, 2010

Captain Jill Hopkins met us at the hotel and presented mother with a flag that was flown over the capitol building in Washington D.C. The flag was accompanied with a certificate in honor of Millicent Peterson Young, a member of theWomen Air Force Service Pilots. Family members watched from the background as the presentation took place.

Senators Kay Bailey Hutchison and Barbara Mikulski had introduced Senate Bill 614 on March 17, 2009, and the president signed it into Public Law 111-40 on July 1, 2009. You could see the pride on the face of Senator Hutchison as she spoke to the honorees. Thanks for all you did Senator Hutchison.

Former WASP Deane Parish "Over 65 years ago we served without any expectations of recognition or glory. We did it with honor, integrity, patriotism, service, faith and commitment. We did it because our country needed us. We thank you for passing this bill to honor our service with the highest honor you can bestow on a civilian!"

This is to certify that the accompanying flag was flown

over the capital of the United States, Washington D.C.
on the 8th of March in the year 2010

This flag was flown in honor of
Millicent Peterson Young
Member of

Women Airforce Service Pilots

First and Foremost

Aircraft Commander   Co-Pilot

1st Helicopter Squadron

60

Senators Kay Bailey
Hutchison and Barbara
Mikulski introduced Senate
Bill 614 on March 17,
2009, and the president
signed it into Public Law
111-40 on July 1, 2009.
You can see the pride on
the faces of Senators
Hutchison and Mikulski
as they addressed the
honorees. Thanks for
all you did Senators.

When the ceremony began, it included the honor guard and the singing of the National Anthem by Master Sergeant Regina Coonrod.

All leadership was involved including the House Majority leader - Nancy Pelosi, Senate Leader Harry Reid, and Minority leader Mitch McConnell.

"Because of the WASP, we dominated in WWII. The WASP were on the cutting edge of flight," said Congressman John Boehner.

"They have brought together Senators Reid & McConnell, Speaker Pelosi & Congressman Boehner to a common cause." ~ Tom Brokaw

Rep. Susan Davis

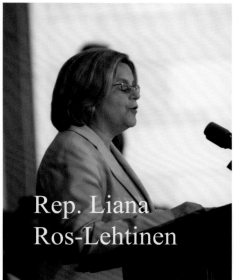

Rep. Liana Ros-Lehtinen

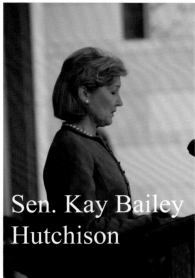

Sen. Kay Bailey Hutchison

Sen Barbara Mikulski

"Honor overdue, because of them women will always be a part of service."

~ Secretary of the Air Force
   Michael Donley

"These remarkable pioneers of the sky paid their own way. We affirm their place in history."

~ Senataor Mitch McConnell

"38 women that died didn't receive suitable honors. Their coffins couldn't even bare the flag of the country for which they served."

~ Senator Hairy Reid

"Once a WASP took to the sky, the world
was never the same!"
        ~Speaker Nancy Pelosi

"Over 65 years ago we served without any expectations of recognition or glory. We did it with honor, integrity, patriotism, service, faith and commitment. We did it because our country needed us. We thank you for passing this bill to honor our service with the highest honor you can bestow on a civilian!"

~ Deane Parish former WASP

83

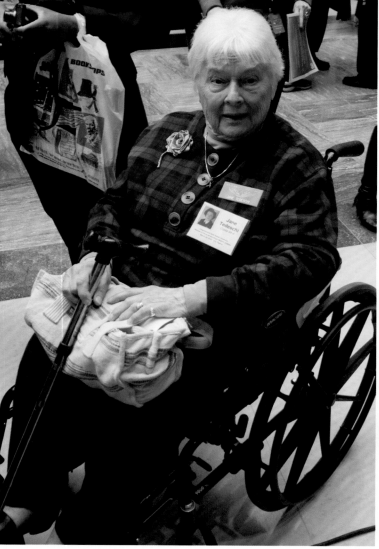

87

Captain Jill Hopkins gives Millicent Amanda Peterson Young her Congressional Gold Medal.

Congressional Gold Medal Recipients
(1776 to Present)

Since the American Revolution, Congress has commissioned gold medals as its highest expression of national appreciation for distinguished achievements and contributions. Each medal honors a particular individual, institution, or event. Although the first recipients included citizens who participated in the American Revolution, the War of 1812 and the Mexican War, Congress broadened the scope of the medal to include actors, authors, entertainers, musicians, pioneers in aeronautics and space, explorers, lifesavers, notables in science and medicine, athletes, humanitarians, public servants, and foreign recipients.

In addition to the requirement that all Congressional Gold Medal legislation must be cosponsored by at least two-thirds (290) of the Members of the House, specific standards are set forth by Rule III (f)(1)(A) of the House Committee on Financial Service's Subcommittee on Domestic Policy and Technology when considering such legislation. Additionally, the Senate Banking, Housing and Urban Affairs Committee requires that at least 67 Senators must cosponsor any Congressional Gold Medal legislation before the committee will consider it.

The primary consideration in giving the Congressional Gold Medal is if the person or persons changed the world.

Recipient(s)	Date of Approval
George Washington	Mar. 25, 1776
Major General Horatio Gates	Nov. 4, 1777
Major General Anthony Wayne	July 26, 1779
Major Henry Lee	Sep. 24, 1779
Brigadier General Daniel Morgan	Mar. 9, 1781
Major General Nathanael Greene	Oct. 29, 1781
John Paul Jones	Oct. 16, 1787
Captain Thomas Truxtun	Mar. 29, 1800
Commodore Edward Preble	Mar. 3, 1805
Captain Isaac Hull, Captain Stephen Decatur, & Captain Jacob Jones	Jan. 29, 1813
Captain William Bainbridge	Mar. 3, 1813
Captain Oliver Hazard Perry & Captain Jesse D. Elliott	Jan. 6, 1814
Lieutenant William Burrows & Lieutenant Edward R. M'Call	Jan. 6, 1814
Captain James Lawrence	Jan. 11, 1814
Captain Thomas MacDonough, Captain Robert Henly, & Lieutenant Stephen Cassin	October 20, 1814

Captain Lewis Warrington	October 21, 1814
Captain Johnson Blakely	November 3, 1814
Major General Jacob Brown	November 3, 1814
Major General Winfield Scott	November 3, 1814
Brigadier General Eleazar W. Ripley, Brigadier General James Miller, and Major General Peter B. Porter	November 3, 1814
Major General Edmund P. Gaines	November 3, 1814
Major General Alexander Macomb	November 3, 1814
Major General Andrew Jackson	February 27, 1815
Captain Charles Stewart	February 22, 1816
Captain James Biddle	February 22, 181
Major General William Henry Harrison & Governor Isaac Shelby	April 4, 1818
Colonel George Croghan	February 13, 1835
Major General Zachary Taylor	July 16, 1846
	March 2, 1847
Rescuers of the Officers & Crew of the U.S. Brig Somers	March 3, 1847
Major General Winfield Scott	March 9, 1848
Major General Zachary Taylor	May 9, 1848
Commander Duncan N. Ingraham	August 4, 1854

Frederick A. Rose	May 11, 1858
Major General Ulysses S. Grant	Dec. 17, 1863
Cornelius Vanderbilt	January 28, 1864
Captain Creighton, Captain Low, and Captain Stouffer	July 26, 1866
Cyrus W. Field	March 2, 1867
George Peabody	March 16, 1867
George F. Robinson	March 1, 1871
Captain Jared S. Crandall & Others	February 24, 1873
John Horn, Jr.	June 20, 1874
	April 28, 1904
John F. Slater	February 5, 1883
Joseph Francis	August 27, 1888
Chief Engineer George Wallace Melville & Others	Sept. 30, 1890
First Lieutenant Frank H. Newcomb	May 3, 1900
First Lieutenant David H. Jarvis, Second Lieutenant Ellsworth P. Bertholf, & Dr. Samuel J. Call	June 28, 1902
Wright Brothers	March 4, 1909
Captain Arthur Henry Rostron	July 6, 1912
Captain Paul H. Kreibohm & Others	March 19, 1914
Domicio da Gama, Romulo S. Naon, & Eduardo Suarez	March 4, 1915

Charles A. Lindbergh	May 4, 1928
Lincoln Ellsworth, Roald Amundsen, & Umberto Nobile	May 29, 1928
Thomas A. Edison	May 29, 1928
First Successful Trans-Atlantic Flight	Feb 9, 1929
Major Walter Reed & Associates for Yellow Fever Experimentations in Cuba	Feb 28, 1929
Officers and Men of the Byrd Antarctic Expedition	May 23, 1930
Lincoln Ellsworth	June 16, 1936
George M. Cohan	June 29, 1936
Mrs. Richard Aldrich & Anna Bouligny	June 20, 1938
Howard Hughes	August 7, 1939
Reverend Francis X. Quinn	August 10, 1939
William Sinnott	June 15, 1940
Roland Boucher	January 20, 1942
George Catlett Marshall, General of the Army, & Fleet Admiral Ernest Joseph King	March 22, 1946
John J. Pershing, General of the Armies of the United States	August 7, 1946
Brigadier General William Mitchell	August 8, 1946
Vice President Alben W. Barkley	August 12, 1949
Irving Berlin	July 16, 1954

Doctor Jonas E. Salk	August 9, 1955
Surviving Veterans of the War Between the States	July 18, 1956
Rear Admiral Hyman George Rickover	August 28, 1958
Doctor Robert H. Goddard	September 16, 1959
Robert Frost	September 13, 1960
Doctor Thomas Anthony Dooley III	May 27, 1961
Bob Hope	June 8, 1962
Sam Rayburn, Speaker of the House of Representatives	September 26, 1962
Douglas MacArthur, General of the Army	October 9, 1962
Walt Disney	May 24, 1968
Winston Churchill	May 7, 1969
Roberto Walker Clemente	May 14, 1973
Marian Anderson	March 8, 1977
Lieutenant General Ira E. Eaker	October 10, 1978
Robert F. Kennedy	November 1, 1978
John Wayne	May 26, 1979
Ben Abruzzo, Maxie Anderson, & Larry Newman	June 13, 1979
Hubert H. Humphrey	June 13, 1979
American Red Cross	December 12, 1979
Ambassador Kenneth Taylor	March 6, 1980
Simon Wiesenthal	March 17, 1980

1980 United States Summer Olympic Team1	July 8, 1980
Queen Beatrix of the Netherlands	March 22, 1982
Admiral Hyman George Rickover	June 23, 1982
Fred Waring	August 26, 1982
Joe Louis	August 26, 1982
Louis L'Amour	August 26, 1982
Leo J. Ryan	Nov. 18, 1983
Danny Thomas	Nov. 29, 1983
Harry S. Truman	May 8, 1984
Lady Bird Johnson	May 8, 1984
Elie Wiesel	May 8, 1984
Roy Wilkins	May 17, 1984
George and Ira Gershwin	August 9, 1985
Anatoly and Avital Shcharansky	May 13, 1986
Harry Chapin	May 20, 1986
Aaron Copland	Sept. 23, 1986
Mary Lasker	Dec. 24, 1987
Jesse Owens	Sept. 20, 1988
Andrew Wyeth	November 9, 1988
Laurence Spelman Rockefeller	May 17, 1990
General Matthew B. Ridgeway	November 5, 1990
General H. Norman Schwarzkopf	April 23, 1991

General Colin Powell	April 23, 1991
Rabbi Menachem Mendel Schneerson	November 2, 1994
Ruth and Billy Graham	February 13, 1996
Francis Albert "Frank" Sinatra	May 14, 1997
Mother Teresa of Calcutta	June 2, 1997
Ecumenical Patriarch Bartholomew	October 6, 1997
Nelson Rolihlahla Mandela	July 29, 1998
Little Rock Nine	October 21, 1998
Gerald R. and Betty Ford	October 21, 1998
Rosa Parks	May 4, 1999
Theodore M. Hesburgh	December 9, 1999
John Cardinal O'Connor	March 3, 2000
Charles M. Schulz	June 20, 2000
Pope John Paul II	July 27, 2000
Ronald and Nancy Reagan	July 27, 2000
Navajo Code Talkers	Dec. 21, 2000
General Henry H. Shelton	January 16, 2002
Prime Minister Tony Blair of the United Kingdom	July 17, 2003
Jackie Roosevelt Robinson	October 23, 2003
Dr. Dorothy Height	Dec. 6, 2003
Reverend Joseph A. DeLaine, Harry and Eliza Briggs, & Levi Pearson	Dec. 15, 2003
Reverend Dr. Martin Luther King, Jr. & Coretta Scott King	October 25 , 2004

The Tuskegee Airmen	April 11 , 2006
Tenzin Gyatso, the Fourteenth Dalai Lama	Sept. 27, 2006
Byron Nelson	October 16, 2006
Dr. Norman E. Borlaug	Dec. 14, 2006
Michael Ellis DeBakey, M.D.	October 10, 2007
Daw Aung San Suu Kyi	May 6, 2008
Constantino Brumidi	July 1, 2008
Edward William Brooke III	July 1, 2008
Native American Code Talkers	October 15, 2008
Women Airforce Service Pilots of WWII (WASP)	July 1, 2009
Neil A. Armstrong, Edwin E. "Buzz" Aldrin, Jr., Michael Collins, and John Herschel Glenn, Jr.	August 7, 2009
Arnold Palmer	Sept. 30, 2009
Muhammad Yunus	October 5, 2010
100th Infantry Battalion, the 442nd Regimental Combat Team, and the Military Intelligence Service	October 8, 2010
Montford Point Marines	Nov. 23, 2011
In honor of the men and women who perished as a result of the terrorist attacks on the United States on September 11, 2001	Dec. 23, 2011
Raoul Wallenberg	July 26, 2012

Addie Mae Collins, Denise McNair,
Carole Robertson, & Cynthia Wesley   May 24, 2013

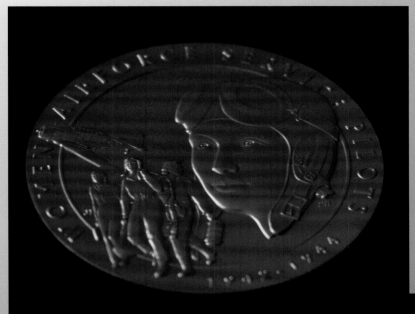

Photos of the front
and back of the
Congressional Gold
Medal issued to the
WASP March 10, 2010

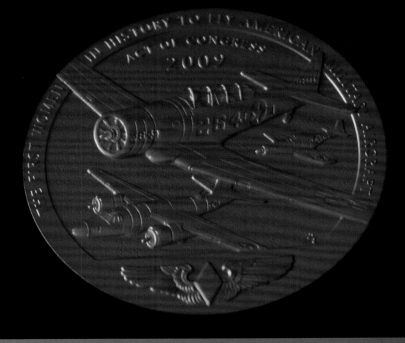

After the ceremony we thought things would quiet down; however, we were stopped on the streets by people wanting to touch mom, thank her, and even cry as they wanted to be near her.

The restaurant created a special menu for the event. It should have read "Congressional Gold Medal," but, you wouldn't believe how many call it the "Congressional Medal of Honor," which is a different medal all together.

We went to dinner with a few friends and they asked mom to make a statement. Soon after she started talking we noticed that the entire restaurant had gone quiet, and at the end everyone applauded. When Millicent Young talks, people listen!

Strangers wanted to be photographed with the WASP.

Two women from WWII chatted with each other at a party held in Millicent's honor. The host invited 20 people the night before thinking that maybe a dozen or so would make it. All of them attended the party as you will see on the next page.

Mom received a warm welcome when she arrives back at the Colorado Springs Airport. Women in the military, men from the VFW and the American Legion were on hand, as well as a number of photographers.

Mom also receives flowers, a coin,
as well as hugs and kisses.

The National Commander of the American Legion came to Colorado Springs to meet personally with Millicent Young shortly after she received the Congressional Gold Medal.

Ola Rexroat, "Sexy Rexy" as her fellow WASP friends call her, showed her Congressional Gold Medal displayed with traditional bead work made by a related Lakota Sioux from the Pine Ridge Reservation. Many Indian Nations have been credited with our victory in World War II.

Dr. Pam Bird was in Washington D.C. during the
Congressional Gold Medal ceremony. When she found
out that the reception had been canceled, she was
upset. Then she went home and told her husband about it
and said she wanted to do something special for the
WASP. The next day, plans were being laid for a very
special event. Pam and Forest Bird created a space in their
museum in Sand Point, Idaho dedicated a park, and launched
a three day party for the WASP later that year. One party included a fly in, car show, history exhibit, bands, food, you
name it, it was there.

The parties included boat rides on Lake Pend Oreille, helicoptor rides, young ladies dressed up as if from the 40's, speeches and book signing. The community was amazing and the Birds' friends pitched in to help, including accomodating some of the WASP and their family members.

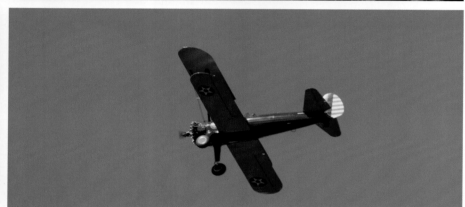

114

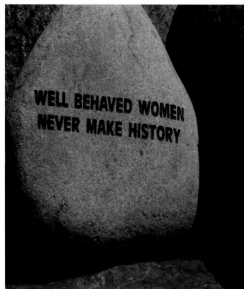

WELL BEHAVED WOMEN NEVER MAKE HISTORY

W ★ A ★ S ★ P

LIFE IS NOT MEASURED
BY THE BREATHS WE TAKE
BUT BY THE MOMENTS THAT
TAKE OUR BREATH AWAY

Women of Courage

Dedicated to the 1,102 pioneering Women Airforce Service Pilots (WASP) who flew bomber, fighter, transport, cargo, drone, liaison and training aircraft in defense of America's freedom in World War II. These female civilian pilots, under the command of the U.S. Army Air Forces, flew more than 60,000,000 miles for their country while facing incredible cultural and gender bias against women in nontraditional roles. The WASP forever changed the role of women in aviation.

Dedicated to the Women Accepted for Volunteer Emergency Service (WAVES), Women's Army Corps (WACS), Women Marines (USMCWR), Women Coast Guard (SPARS), Army Nurse Corps, Navy Nurse Corps, the civilian women (Rosie the Riveters) and others who have made significant contributions to our military- past, present and future.

We honor all who have lived a life of dedication to their local communities and country. We thank those women who have paved the way for others in all walks of life by contributing to humanity and have "made a difference."

The next party took place at Cafe Regis in Red Lodge, Montana. It was a celebration of the Gold Medals with my mother being the guest of honor. The other gold medals were won by a septuagenarian athlete.

The Rocky Mountain Air Show just outside of Denver was the next stop on the trip. Millicent Young and Kathryn Gunderson were interviewed. Below they posed with artist Christopher Manzanares.

Sunday, October 3, 2010, the WASP go to The Dole Institute of Politics where they received the Dole Leadership Prize. The WASP were taken for flights, had speaking engagements, and were fed very well. It was a fun event. Bob Dole could't attend as he was recovering from hip problems.

118

Millicent Young received
recognition at Peterson
Air Force Base in
Colorado Springs.

Induction into the Nebraska Aviation Hall of Fame.

Denver recognized the WASP at various events.

The WASP are always a hit at Women in Aviation
International.

Millicent Amanda Peterson Young was the first female Grand Marshal for the Colorado Springs Veteran's Day Parade.

The WASP at Avenger Field in Sweetwater, Texas for the ground breaking of the upgrades to the WASP museum. Tell me these women in their late 80's and 90's are not full of energy!

After Sweetwater, the WASP go to Pecan Plantation, where they are treated to some flights. How many of you would fly in a plane with no fuselage? Many of the WASP jumped at a chance. These photos are of my mother's turn.

A young man assists WASP in preparing for their flight in a Stearman. All the WASP have been flying in these plains 60 + years before he was born.

Special Thanks to:

My family for all their love and support.

All of Congress & the President of the United States for providing recognition to the WASP.

Pamela & Forrest Bird, as well as all their staff, & community. What an amazing party and recognition!

The Pucci family for opening their home to me and taking care of our dog Honey.

The Robert Dole Institute, their staff and friends that gave recognition to the WASP with the Leadership Award.

All the WASP for being the Women of Courage! - *William A. Young II.*

Millicent Amanda Peterson Young WASP 44 - W 10.

Sitting on the wing of an AT6 at the Pima Air Museum just outside of Tucson, AZ.

You should have seen the 18 year old docent as mom took off her oxygen, laid down her blind cane, and proceeded to climb on the wing of this plane. He was on his way to stop her as another older docent stopped him and told him these women can do what ever they want!